Advance Praise for *After:*

"*After*, by Chelsea Harrison, is a warm cup of tea or hot cocoa on a snowy winter day. It's a night swim with your lover, hoping you won't get caught, but thrilled to be together. It's the pit you feel in your stomach after a terrible loss that slowly heals, but never truly goes away. It's the fire of finding yourself again, and of healing. It's the memories that still sting, but remind us of who we are and where we've been. It's new becomings and new life."
—Hillary Gonzalez, author of *Seasons*

"Chelsea Harrison has eyes. And a heart. Plainly, she's on a walkabout to sort out anything & everything beautiful & beastly along the cranky tightrope called life. But it's the seeing 'and understanding' that counts. And after all, as we discover, it's a great life, innit?"
—Professor Mike Olmert, University of Maryland, College Park; Emmy award-winning television, film and print writer

AFTER

Chelsea Harrison

Copyright © 2025 Chelsea Harrison

All Rights Reserved. This book or any portion thereof may not be reproduced, in whole or in part, in any form (beyond that permitted by Sections 107 and 108 of the U.S Copyright Law and except by reviewers for the public press), without the express written permission of the publisher except for the use of brief quotations in a book review.

Harrison, Chelsea / author

After / Chelsea Harrison

Poems

ISBN: 979-8-9869524-7-5

Edited by: Beth Gordon
Book Design: Amanda McLeod
Cover Art: Chelsea Harrison / Evgen_Prozhyrko via iStock
Cover Design: Amanda McLeod

PUBLISHER
Femme Salve Books
Asheville, NC
www.femmesalvebooks.net
www.animalheartpress.net

LRPJ- For you, from you, about you. It's always you.

Table of Contents

Prose Poem for the Future	9
AFTER LOVE	11
Bounds Green	12
Beyond	13
For Dominic	14
At Cornfield Creek	15
And I was left standing here with these small hands	16
Runes	17
What do you want him to do?	18
AFTER LOSS	19
Tricklexodus	20
It's Not About the Waving	21
Roots	22
Sometime in June	23
The Queen of Swords	24
Gideon	25
Up	26
This is not an elegy	27
When the World Ends	28
AFTER BIRTH	29
Invocation	30
How to Swaddle	31
Thick	33
So Sayeth the Bee	34
My daughter, topless at the beach	36
Oh you have a life, haha	37

The Child that Came	38
Remedy	39
I cradle your head and	40
Acknowledgements	41
About the Author	43

Prose Poem for the Future

Once upon a time, and for thousands of years,
the world was ruled by men and the Men thought that they
were Gods. The angry Men played fast
and loose with the lives of other Men, and they played
war games and launched weapons at each other,
as did the Gods, in the stories of ancient times.
In the very worst of times, Men lorded their power
over women and children, blatantly and without shame.
The richer and more powerful the Men became,
the more corrupt they became
and the greedier they became for more wealth and more power.
The women and children feared for their lives
because of the weapons and the violence and greed of Men.
It was a truly dark time.

The age of man begat the age of women.

The age of women was the natural answer to the darkness and fear of the age of man. The women knew in their bones that it was their time and they began to lead, in small ways at first, then toppling the worst men from their pedestals, that were built on the backs of the downtrodden and persecuted. The women took their rightful places in the halls of justice, leadership, and religion. Women climbed the mountains and from this new height, they could see what needed to be done, and more importantly, they could see each other, each on her mountaintop, ready to work. The women ruled with compassion, logic, and virtue. The women thought, *why didn't we do this sooner?*

But the women never forgot the dark days behind them. They invented peace out of chaos. They reinvented truth. They invested in love. They nurtured compromise.

The women believed, and it was thus.

AFTER LOVE

Bounds Green

The autumn air was crisp—
like something about to happen
and leaves crunched underfoot
something you meant to say.

We stood face forward against the winter
hand in hand not knowing
what the whitewash would bring.

Each seasonal kaleidoscope
we learn a new dance
write a new book
examine the possibilities.

feathers falling through air

I will follow the smoke from your chimney
until there is nothing left to burn.

Beyond

I shall find you in the next life
ages and ages hence

I shall seek and shall find you
and plant myself into your life

Next time, I won't take no
for an answer and I won't
question the universe anymore

or doubt that she cut us from the same cloth,
twisted us apart from the same loaf,
split us asunder from the same dying ember

the same cosmic burst created you and I,
that we in turn, create

For Dominic

You, on stage, me, in the audience
At the premiere run of History Boys
I swear, I will swear it-
our eyes locked, you smiled and winked.

At the premiere run of History Boys
maybe you winked at all the girls-
our eyes locked, you smiled and winked.
Dakin, cheeky Dakin, to the last.

Maybe you winked at all the girls-
but today it is me, blushing
Dakin, cheeky Dakin to the last.
An act I will play over and over, a young girl's pride.

But today it is me blushing
Remembering the silent applause, our unspoken moment.
An act I will play over and over, a young girl's pride.
You on stage, me in the audience.

At Cornfield Creek

I. Summer
The tide flows like lines in a song
sun touches everything
(even our hearts)—
waves of heat and promise.
Take comfort in the
shade of the tall oak,
the oak that has waited just for this.

II. Fall
The water moves like a sip of tea
Gold to yellow to brown
the trees remind us that
change must come.
Some things remain the same.

III. Winter
The river dances like oil paint.
The world slips on her wedding dress
white and more white
Two tiny flakes cling to this window
and melt together.
Soft, silent, waiting.

IV. Spring
Finally. We gather together
for love, laughter, life.
The river flows like
wind chimes and nesting begins.
Everything green and alive
birds, flowers, trees.

Love—brought back to life.

And I was left standing here with these small hands

At your wedding, you took my hand, jokingly
to see if there was a diamond there yet.

And you said,
"You have such small hands.
I seem to remember that about you."
You put my palm to yours to see-

(and I was shocked at how quickly my body
could crack and crumble into dry desert earth,
and I lay like a pile of dirt at your feet, and then I felt
the invisible gut punch- a frozen bowling ball;
then I watched the torrent of tears stream down my
face and over the dock, causing the tide to rise
and my heart just stopped and stared, blood
stood still and helpless in its veins and
I whispered to you every secret I've ever known,
every lie I ever told, every detail of the heartache I felt-
I whispered to you, "I still…)

I smiled shyly and laughed.
And just like that,
you were called away by your new wife,
by your new life.

Runes

Once we had a couple's Runes reading
you pulled a Loki rune
and somehow that became our nickname
for your boss.
"How's Loki today?"
I would ask in a text.
"Fine haha" you'd reply.
Once you said,
"shh don't wake her"
which was unusually clever for you.

So when I found out
you were fucking her
it was even funnier
the chaos that followed
in your wake.

What do you want him to do?

Leathered tanned hide, whiskers bristling against
bony fingers as you stroke the frown of lonely years.
Crouching in dark corners of wooden sheds and stone caves
the only light you see is yellow and tinged.
The bread you eat is all crust.
The air you breathe is first exhaled by bats.
Even the fish take pity on you.
Each moment bleeds into the next with no hope
no hope of disruption or contact.
Maybe your eyes are watery and bulging.
Maybe you use an old sail as a blanket.
Maybe no one knows where to visit you.

And the only melody that finds you is- what have I done, what have I done?

I picture you thus and am satisfied.

AFTER LOSS

Tricklexodus

The world is getting smaller now
for those of us left–
when the galaxy yawned and swallowed
so many, like Jonah
without intention, or even knowledge, who knew
we would need to be survivors again.

Is there a type of exodus that isn't
mass, like just a trickle but very steady?
Tricklexodus–
sounds like the next big thing.
And will it stop?
Some of them just want to keep dying and dying.

There's a moth at the window just now
wings beating the glass, up and up,
like an evangelical in prayer.

And when it knew it could not reach the light,
dove back again, swallowed into dark.

It's Not About the Waving

After Stevie Smith
After Maggie Smith

Watching from a distance as you hurl yourself into wave after wave not
desperate but nearly, moonlight wavering, waving
in your shadow, not grasping the fine line you cross, not wanting to but
admitting- it's not so rare a thing- drowning.

And I ask myself- is it the
wild, reckless pleasure of swimming in moonlight
that calls you? Or something darker– the call of
deeper, deeper, darkness– in the end, both enough to put out that life.

Roots

Every time I
loose the roots
of potted plants,
I think of you.

Gently tickling
the soft tendrils
shuffling off the old
dirt for new.

I think of you at
the smell of mulch
the sounds of certain birds
Snapdragons
and when you showed
me how to gently pinch
their jaws to watch
the fire come out.

Even now
we are in communion
root and flower
memory and breeze
past and future.

I think of you now—
what work are you doing?
what soil are you turning?

Sometime in June

I went to a baseball game and got drunk
the day you died.

I couldn't watch you die,
not like the others
not this time.

I was drinking Coors Light while
you were high on morphine.
Here's hoping you were more satisfyingly numb.

It was the Angels and Orioles,
we lost
and baseball will never be the same.

I lost my grief in the shouting crowds,
the cracking bats and the crawling Baltimore train
back to home.

I'm not sure if I loved you enough,
Your Fair-Weather Granddaughter.

The Angels won that day and I hope you got your glass of milk.

The Queen of Swords

The Queen of Swords refuses to buy what they are selling.
She knows about that butterfly perched on the end of her sword,
but she is looking beyond it, wary of some danger.
She knows the pink-and-purple cape is some bullshit.

But her crown is simple–thick, gold, and strong
Lapis Lazuli like the dusky sky,
that is her real cloak.

They say she is intolerant,
with a narrow outlook on life.
They say she's not empathetic.
She wears no make-up, no jewels, and pants.

What a double-edged life she must lead.
Queen–Female–Sword–Butterfly

She is done with tolerance.
She is done with nurturing,
empathy, compromise, archetype.
She has a sword
and she knows how to use it.

Gideon

There were no rainbows—
hardly any light to refract
there was the mottled green of your eyes, still open
there was the emptiness

Why do we use rainbows
to tidy up death this way?

Isn't it enough to say
goodbye, old friend
see you again, my familiar
easy passage, wild spirit
 to weep, to mourn,
 to contemplate the mystery?

What if there is no bridge, no rainbow?

Sometimes, though, when you were asleep
the mid-morning sun alighting on your fur
and the beams would filter through each
brown tiger hair and shine
like a rainbow.

Up

Assume we know nothing.
Like that time we drove
the Bay Bridge in terrible fog.
I thought we were going down
and you thought still up.
Really there was no way to tell.
Like an airplane, you said,
and we both thought of falling.

Assume it's all more complex than we imagine.
Assume we're not alone.
Assume energy and sound and love and tides
are what it's all about.

Of course souls are recycled, of course.
Of course magic is real, dear.
Of course you must keep going on and on.

Assume your power and assume pain.
Suspend disbelief.
Assume we know nothing
that hasn't already been known.

This is not an elegy

This is not an elegy
because elegies are forlorn, still, bereft
and you never were.

You were bright and warm,
vibrant like a purple sunset,
shining in the light and in the dark.

You were in the world and of it.
You were the energy of the ocean-
at once calm and strong.

Don't say elegy.
Say celebrate, tribute, cherish, remember.

Sing: *Celebrate we will,*
For life is short but sweet for certain.

Not silence, not stillness
but laughter (and what a great laugh).

Write, instead, about what we lived for,
what we were born for,
what extraordinary love we found.

This is not an elegy.
This is not the end

When the World Ends

Look for dirt being blown into the air.
Dead vegetation in an otherwise green area.
Look for dry parched earth in an otherwise moist area.

You may also see fire coming from the ground
or appearing to burn above the ground
or appearing to burn in mid-air.

Near water, look for water that boils
in an otherwise cool area. Look for
water being blown into the air.
Listen for roaring, blowing, hissing.

Look for your doppelgänger walking
towards you out of the forest, naked, expressionless.
You may also see orbs of radiant light.

Look for kindness in an otherwise hostile area,
common ground in a sinking landscape.
Listen for major chords, angelic sighing, and wings flapping.

In the air, notice that it tastes like spun sugar,
notice the earth shrinking
and that blue and green become one.

AFTER BIRTH

Invocation

Mother,
Here I am, ready.
I am smoldering, molting, shedding,
washed ashore
from the living flesh.

I am in an ancient cave
whose walls are slick and red.
I am on a cloud,
and see everything.
I am flickering, flickering, flickering.
I am just below the surface, unseen.
I am all places and nowhere.

Mother–
I am ready to soar in the moonlight,
to burn my own fuel,
to taste the salt of my own tears.
Lower me down onto dirt, sand, or stone.

Be joyful,
for I have swum an endless ocean to find you.
Be a brave burning woman now, momma,
and we will walk the Earth hand in hand.

Be calm,
and never doubt the depth of your own strength.

Ready now,
my sweet momma?

I am here.

How to Swaddle
(after W. Berry)

i.

Make a place for baby.
Place baby there.
Smooth the soft blanket.
Notice its thickness and shape.
Triangulate the blanket.
It won't be a perfect triangle.
It doesn't matter.
Try to get comfortable with that.

ii.

As if conducting the softest part
of the song, lift baby onto blanket,
one hand under neck, one
supporting rump. Notice the two
tiny white orbs, full of everything primal,
learning and forgetting each instant.
There are no perfect moments,
but this comes close.
Recognize the present moment.

iii.

Choose a corner, cross and tuck.
Curl the bottom folds over ten tiny toes.
Final corner, cross and tuck;
complete the woven hug.
Choose an adorable metaphor-
burrito, cocoon, angel.
Elevate burrito cocoon angel into your arms.
Be prepared for your swaddle
to come untucked momentarily.

Whisper or sing. Pray or laugh.
Out of these infinite actions,
accept what comes.

Thick

Momma wants to tell you,
Thick is good.
Thick be like
gravy, ice cream, syrup.
Thick be like
a room full of women laughing,
like digging deep in the sand and
squeezing as hard as you can.
Thick like a book
full of stories where she slays the dragons.
Thick like baby cheeks,
like a snowman's bottom–
millions of crystal flakes rolled into
something solid.
Thick like the fog after the rain,
weaving around streetlights.
Don't let anybody tell you
thick ain't the thing–
strong, rooted, stable as hell
spread it on
thick as my love.

So Sayeth the Bee

I.
"In nearly every species, a male bee's only job is to mate with a female."*

I have often wondered about
the ancestral buzzing inside your mind.
The empty hum calling you
insert
repeat
generations, through time and space
survival-cum-evolution

When does spirit enter into it?
Fathers and sons and sons, my sons
will have more than one job.

II.
"Most male bees do not even have the structures necessary to make wax or carry pollen, so males in social species cannot contribute to the daily work that goes on in the hive."

Helpless, hapless males
some might say–
the weaker sex.
What do they do while they are not
contributing to the daily work, these bees?
Sit and watch?
Kick back in an armchair?
Play golf?
Impatiently think about
fucking some more?
They cannot help it,
so sayeth the bee.

III.

"In fact, female honeybees usually force surviving males out of the nest before winter or when food becomes scarce."

I am reminded of how my grandmother
tuts and shuffles around
my grandfather when he comes in
"her kitchen."

Is this where spirit enters into it?
Evolution-plus-love
cocoon, hearth, warmth.
Such love was there,
never winter, never scarcity.

*Italicized excerpts from "How Bees Work" Tracy V. Wilson

My daughter, topless at the beach

Go ahead girl.
Do it while you can.
Feel the sun on the full
spread of your back,
while your chest is
just a chest,
while your bliss is
easy and buoyant.
All things being equal
between you and your brothers.

The sun glistens on your skin like a pearl.
Windswept, you look out to the ocean,
spread your arms wide,
run wild like your curls.
Scream like you own the place.

Oh you have a life, haha

I have/had many lives.
Many lives in a day
many days in a moment
several lives out of one life.

Let me start again.

As parents, we are dealing with
shit and tears on a daily basis.
What other life requires that?
Muses? Nurses? Prison guards? Depressed zookeepers?

Before these lives, there was only one.
But I know it must be this way.
I know that before they
sprang from me, leaping like
ballerinas, braying like a conch song,
my children were four
bony, wet little spirits
crowded and crouched
around a single white
candle in the
spiral's
apex.

The Child that Came

The child that came
was ancient like Jasper
fluid like pebbles
and clear as the truth.

The child had legs for marching
laughter like sunlight
and wise, ageless eyes.

The child came on an indigo night
with a cornsilk moon
and a green buzzing wind.

The child might have come silently
on horseback
or pulled up to shore
on a small boat.

The child chose her
for her ancient energy
her no-nonsense
and her still pools of light.

Remedy

When I think of your soul,
I think of the galaxy.
The black depth of your eyes
echoed in the starry unknown.

And you are 5,
so I am wondering how to tell you
that magic is real and it's in you.

You believe now–but will you?
Or will it fade and have to be
reignited, like your Ma?

It can be hard– living
in the galaxy. The dark
in all its beauty
can still be dark.

But I will hold your hand as long as you'll let me.
And I will help you listen to those ancient voices we both hear.
And I will sit with you in the dark,
waiting for the stars to come back.

I cradle your head and
after John Ashbery

I cradle your head in my palm and
somehow my love for you
makes me angry at the world.
My love is as impotent as the fog.
The world will always reach us,
the bullhorn in the night.

Is it enough?
Is it enough to bare body, bone, blood,
breast to give you life?
Is it enough to think of you always, to feel
your movements like a ghost limb?
Will it be enough?

And yet, here in the shadows between sun and moon,
pulsing body to pulsing body,
through your feathered breathing
I hear a whisper of faith,
I feel an aching, weepy surety—
my furious love stands a chance.

Acknowledgements

"Prose Poem for the Future" originally appeared in *InJoy Magazine*; and later appeared in *From the Ashes* (Animal Heart Press).

"Oh you have a life, haha" and "Thick" were originally published in *From the Ashes* (Animal Heart Press).

"This is not an elegy" p. 25 - the line *Celebrate we will because life is short but sweet for certain* is a lyric from the song "Two-Step" by Dave Matthews.

About the Author

Chelsea is a mom of four and proud Marylander. She is also Editor in Chief of Annapolis Moms Media and a writing tutor and professor for two local colleges. Chelsea earned her Master's degree at Durham University (UK) in English Language & Literature with a focus in poetry. In her free time, she enjoys reading, crafting, baking, or watching a movie with the little wildlings.

Visit Chelsapeakecreative.com to find out more about Chelsea's publications and other professional adventures.

www.ingramcontent.com/pod-product-compliance
Lightning Source LLC
Chambersburg PA
CBHW060224050426
42446CB00013B/3164